Beyond the Science Lab

A Celebration of God and Science
by Jason Lindsey, a.k.a. "Mr. Science"

Pinwheel Books

Pinwheel Books

Beyond The Science Lab, A Celebration of God and Science
Text copyright © 2012 by Jason Lindsey
Illustrations copyright © 2012 by Ashley MacLure and MartinaVaculikova

Published by Pinwheel Books
Brookline, MA
www.pinwheelbooks.com

ISBN 978-0-985-4248-48
Library of Congress Control Number: 2012954168

For Lena, the best wife ever and my little

scientists Conner, Ethan, Brynna and Madigan.

J.L.

Table of Contents

Dear Parents and Educators

Kids can ask what seems like a thousand tough questions a day. As a parent of four kids under the age of nine I have heard just about everything from, "Why do I have freckles?" to "Why does my head hurt when I eat ice cream?" As a strong Christian, I wanted to not only answer these questions accurately but to utilize the opportunity to inform my children that God is the ultimate force behind all these mysteries. That's why I developed the experiment series, **Beyond the Science Lab**, which takes kids beyond the beakers and Bunsen burners and shows them that God is the ultimate scientist.

The hands-on activities in this book will allow you to use science to teach God's awesome word. You do not have to be a rocket scientist to do these experiments and most of the ingredients can be found right at home or in the classroom. You can watch the Beyond the Science Lab television segment on the TCT Television Network during children's programming each Saturday. To learn more about the children's programming on the TCT Television Network go to www.tctkids.tv.

Be aware that kids will ask questions throughout each experiment because they are curious. You want to encourage these questions. It may sound like too many at times, but realize these questions help children become strong thinkers.

Please, don't let the science intimidate you. Grab the Bible, the ingredients, and the kids for an out-of-this-world experience that will not only get everyone Hooked on Science, but also get everyone Hooked on Jesus.

For even more Beyond The Science Lab fun, and to watch videos of the experiments in this book, visit http://hookedonscience.org/beyondthesciencelab.

I would like to acknowledge Sherry Cook, cocreator of the Quirkles; Doug Jenkins, a retired science educator, and Mark Anderson, a pastor at Lynwood Baptist church in Cape Girardeau, MO, for reviewing this book.

"Grab the Bible, the ingredients, and the kids for an out of this world experience that will not only get everyone Hooked on Science, but also get everyone Hooked on Jesus."

Science Safety

Each **Beyond the Science Lab** experiment is safe to perform with an adult present. Please follow these safety precautions when doing any science experiment:

ALWAYS have an adult present.

ALWAYS wear the correct safety gear while doing any experiment.

NEVER eat or drink anything when performing any experiment. The reason for this is that some of the substances used in the experiments could be harmful to your health if accidentally ingested, which is more likely if you are eating or drinking during the experiments.

Some experiments in this book require balloons and other objects that could become a choking hazard. To be safe, adults should be the ones performing the experiments involving these objects. Children can choke or suffocate on uninflated or broken balloons, so please keep uninflated or broken balloons away from children!

Safety Symbols

Throughout the book, you will find a number of symbols which should remind you to take special precautions. Study them now so you can remember what they mean when you do each experiment:

Clothing Safety
Substances used could stain or burn clothing.

Fire Safety
Care should be taken around open flames.

Electrical Safety
Care should be taken when using electrical equipment.

Fume Safety
Chemicals could cause dangerous fumes.

Thermal Safety
Use caution when handling hot objects.

Sharp Safety
Danger of cuts or punctures.

Eye Safety
Danger to the eye; safety goggles should be worn.

Chemical Safety
Chemicals can cause burns or are poisonous if absorbed through the skin.

Experiment Supply List

This is a list of supplies you will need for each **Beyond the Science Lab** experiment. Most of these supplies can be found around the house or at your local department store. You can purchase a neodymium magnet online.

1. Soaring Toilet Paper

Leaf blower, toilet paper, 12-inch wooden dowel rod.

2. Film Canister Rockets

Empty 35mm film canister with snap-on lid,
water, Alka-Seltzer tablet.

3. The Collapsing Can

Empty soda can, hot plate, bowl, water, ice, tongs.

4. Soda Can Science

Can of non-diet soda.

5. Squeaky Clean Science

Ivory soap, microwave oven.

6. Disappearing Color

Two clear drinking glasses, water, blue food coloring, bleach, stirrer.

7. Air Cannon

Five-gallon bucket, rubber mat, two long heavy duty zip ties,
scissors and knife.

8. Skewer a Balloon

Balloon, skewer.

9. Magnetic Money

Neodymium magnet, United States one dollar bill.

10. Cup of Sounds

Plastic cup, sponge, string, water, scissors.

11. Cloud in a Bottle

Two-liter clear plastic bottle, water, matches.

12. Newton's Tablecloth

Several heavy glass dishes, a tablecloth without a hem, a square table with an edge.

13. Dry Water

Water, ice cube tray.

Ready, Set, Go!

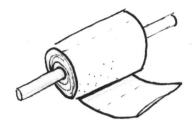

God Gives Us Strength

BIBLE TRUTH: *God gives us strength to do things we never imagined.*

WHAT THE BIBLE SAYS: *Job 5:9*

9 He performs wonders that cannot be fathomed, miracles that cannot be counted.

HANDS-ON EXPERIMENT: Soaring Toilet Paper

Ingredients:

Leaf blower
Toilet paper
Twelve-inch wooden dowel rod

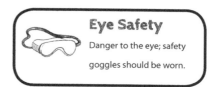

Eye Safety
Danger to the eye; safety
goggles should be worn.

Instructions:

STEP 1: Put the 12-inch wooden dowel rod through the toilet paper and unroll a few pieces of tissue.

STEP 2: Hold the dowel rod horizontally so the roll will unroll away from you.

STEP 3: Ask an adult to turn on the leaf blower and to aim the stream of air over the top surface of the roll of toilet paper.

Explanation

Bernoulli's Principle states that the pressure exerted by a fluid decreases as its velocity increases. Just like water, air is considered a fluid. Increasing the velocity over the top surface of the toilet paper lowers the pressure of the air pushing down on the paper. The paper is lifted because there is now an unbalanced force of air pressure acting upward.

Bible Connection

Just as the strong air flowing from the leaf blower gives strength to the toilet paper, God gives us strength to do things we never imagined.

Science Terms

Bernoulli's Principle: Bernoulli's principle states that the pressure exerted by a fluid decreases as its velocity increases.

High Pressure System: A high-pressure system or an anticyclone is an area where the air diverges and sinks. A high-pressure system usually brings clear skies.

Low Pressure System: A low-pressure system or cyclone is an area where the air converges and rises. A low-pressure system usually brings precipitation.

SCIENCE QUIZ

1) Define Bernoulli's principle, high pressure system and low pressure system.

2) What happened when you increased the velocity over the top surface of the toilet paper?

3) Why is the toilet paper lifted?

God's Power

BIBLE TRUTH: *From amazing sunsets to majestic landscapes, we see God's power everywhere.*

WHAT THE BIBLE SAYS: *Psalm 47:2*

2. For the Lord Most High is awesome, the great King over all the Earth.

HANDS-ON EXPERIMENT: Film Canister Rockets

Ingredients:

Empty 35mm film canister with snap-on lid
Water
Alka-Seltzer tablet
Safety goggles

Eye Safety
Danger to the eye; safety
goggles should be worn.

Instructions:

STEP 1: Pour water into the 35 mm film canister until it is half full.

STEP 2: Place the Alka-Seltzer tablet into the empty 35mm film canister, snap on the lid and quickly flip it upside-down so the lid is on the table.

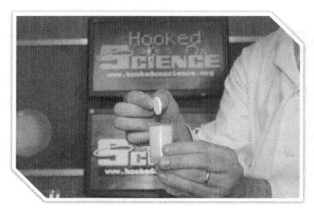 

STEP 3: Stand away from the table and observe.

Explanation

Carbon dioxide gas is produced as a result of a chemical reaction between the water and Alka-Seltzer tablet. Alka-Seltzer, an over-the-counter medication, is used as a pain reliever. When mixed with water, the ingredients in Alka-Seltzer—citric acid and sodium bicarbonate—make it fizz. The gas builds up pressure until there is enough force to launch the 35mm film canister into the air.

Bible Connection

Just as the carbon dioxide gas gives the film canister enough power to launch it into the air, God gives us power. From amazing sunsets to majestic landscapes, we witness His power every day.

Science Term

Carbon Dioxide – Carbon dioxide is a colorless, odorless gas that animals breathe out and is naturally found in the air.

SCIENCE QUIZ

1) Define carbon dioxide.

2) Which gas is produced when you place the Alka-Seltzer tablet into water?

3) What launched the film canister into the air?

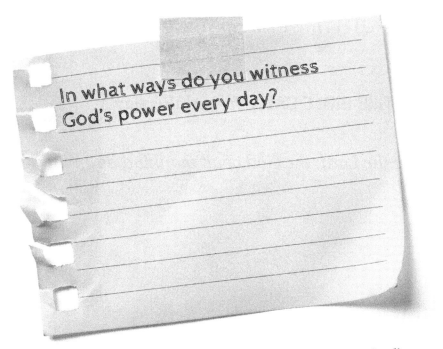

In what ways do you witness God's power every day?

God's Strength

BIBLE TRUTH: *There isn't anything too hard for God.*

WHAT THE BIBLE SAYS: *Jeremiah 32:27*

27 I am the Lord, the God of all mankind. Is anything too hard for me?

HANDS-ON EXPERIMENT: The Collapsing Can

Ingredients:

Empty soda can
Hot plate
Bowl
Water
Ice
Tongs

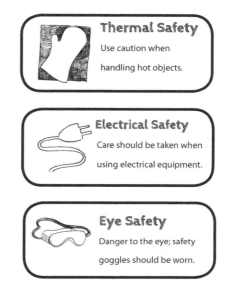

Thermal Safety
Use caution when handling hot objects.

Electrical Safety
Care should be taken when using electrical equipment.

Eye Safety
Danger to the eye; safety goggles should be worn.

Instructions:

STEP 1: Fill the bowl with ice and water.

STEP 2: Place one tablespoon of water into the empty soda can. Ask an adult to turn on the hot plate to a high setting, and place the soda can on the hot plate. DO NOT touch the hot plate! Touching the hot plate can cause a serious burn.

STEP 3: Wait a few minutes for water vapor to appear above the can. Use the tongs to grasp the sides of the can.

STEP 4: Quickly flip the can and dip it immediately into the cold water.

Explanation

When the can is turned upside down and submerged into the cold water, the water inside the can goes from the gas state (water vapor) to a liquid state, and the pressure decreases. Now that the air pressure on the outside is stronger, the can is crushed.

Bible Connection

Just as it wasn't too hard for the air to crush the can, there isn't anything too hard for God. God makes things happen even when we think it is impossible.

Science Terms

Air – Air is the mixture of gases that surrounds the earth.

High Pressure System - A high-pressure system or an anticyclone is an area where the air diverges and sinks. A high-pressure system usually brings clear skies.

Low Pressure System - A low-pressure system or cyclone is an area where the air converges and rises. A low-pressure system usually brings precipitation.

SCIENCE QUIZ

1) Define air, high pressure system and low pressure system.

2) Why did the can crush when you dipped the can into the icy water?

Rejoice

BIBLE TRUTH: *When we accept Jesus, God expects us to get excited and to rejoice.*

WHAT THE BIBLE SAYS: *Matthew 5:12*

12 Rejoice and be glad, because great is your reward in heaven, for in the same way they persecuted the prophets who were before you.

HANDS-ON EXPERIMENT: Soda Can Science

Ingredients:

One can of non-diet soda.

Eye Safety

Danger to the eye; safety goggles should be worn.

Instructions:

STEP 1: Rapidly shake the can to excite the carbon dioxide gas bubbles inside the soda can.

STEP 2: Tap the side of the can several times.

STEP 3: Open the soda can and observe!

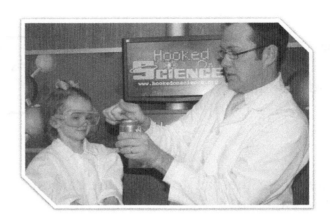

Explanation

By tapping the side of the can you dislodge the carbon dioxide bubbles from the walls of the can. This causes the bubbles to travel to the top of the can. Upon opening the can the carbon dioxide bubbles rush out of the can. The soda stays in the can instead of spraying everywhere!

Bible Connection

The tapping represents God tapping us, encouraging us to accept his son, Jesus Christ, into our hearts. When we accept Jesus into our hearts, we are expected to get as excited as the carbon dioxide bubbles in a dropped can of soda.

Science Term

Carbon Dioxide – Carbon dioxide is a colorless, odorless gas that animals breathe out and is naturally found in the air.

SCIENCE QUIZ

1) Define carbon dioxide.

2) How did you dislodge the carbon dioxide bubbles from the wall of the can to the top of the can?

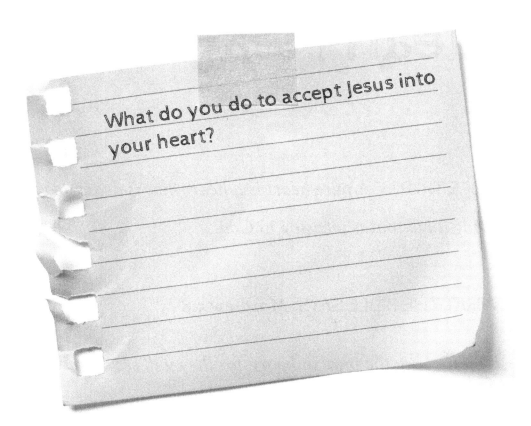

What do you do to accept Jesus into your heart?

Squeaky Clean Heart

BIBLE TRUTH: *A pure heart is a heart that is dedicated to living a life that is pleasing to God.*

WHAT THE BIBLE SAYS: *Matthew 5:8*

8 Blessed are the pure in heart, for they will see God.

HANDS-ON EXPERIMENT: Squeaky Clean Science

Ingredients:

Ivory Soap
Microwave oven

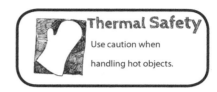

Instructions:

STEP 1: Place one bar of Ivory Soap on a microwave-safe dish and put it into the microwave oven.

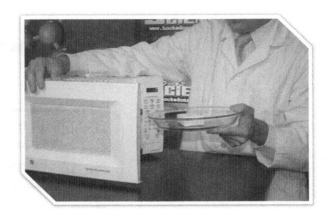

STEP 2: Heat the soap for one minute and observe.

Explanation

The heat causes the air molecules inside the soap to get excited. When this occurs the soap expands into an incredible size.

Bible Connection

God expects us to have a heart that is as pure as Ivory soap and that expands to an incredible size as it fills with the love of God.

Science Term

Air -Air is the mixture of gases that surrounds the earth.

SCIENCE QUIZ

1) Define air.

2) What happens when the air molecules are heated in the Ivory soap?

What do you do to keep a squeaky clean heart?

God's Light

BIBLE TRUTH: *Let God's light shine brightly through you, otherwise the world will fill the void with darkness.*

WHAT THE BIBLE SAYS: *1 John 1:5*

5 This is the message we have heard from him and declare to you: God is light; in him there is no darkness at all.

34

HANDS-ON EXPERIMENT: Disappearing Color

Ingredients:

Two clear drinking glasses
Water
Blue food coloring
Bleach
Stirrer

Fume Safety
Chemicals could cause dangerous fumes.

Clothing Safety
Substances used could stain or burn clothing.

Eye Safety
Danger to the eye; safety goggles should be worn.

Instructions:

STEP 1: Fill each drinking glass half-way with water.

STEP 2: Mix two drops of the blue food coloring into each drinking glass.

STEP 3: Have an adult mix about three tablespoons of bleach into one of the drinking glasses.

STEP 4: Carefully stir the water in the glass with the bleach.

Explanation

The bleach reacts with the chromophores in the water molecules. The chromophore is the part of the molecule that gives an object color. The bleach shortens the length of the chromophores in the water molecules. When this happens, the molecules absorb light and the color disappears.

36

Bible Connection

You were able to change the color of the water from blue back to transparent by adding bleach. When this happens the light shines through for all to see. If we don't let God shine brightly through our lives the world will fill the void with darkness.

Science Terms

Chromophore- A chromophore is the part of a molecule responsible for its color.

Molecule - A molecule is made up of two or more atoms that are joined together.

SCIENCE QUIZ

1) Define chromophore and molecule.

2) Which part of the molecule causes an object to have color?

3) What shortened the length of the chromophore?

The Holy Spirit

BIBLE TRUTH: *We can't see or touch the Holy Spirit but we can feel his presence in our hearts.*

WHAT THE BIBLE SAYS: *Matthew 28:20*

20 Teaching them to obey everything I have commanded you. And surely I am with you always, to the very end of the age.

HANDS-ON EXPERIMENT: Air Cannon

Ingredients:

One five-gallon bucket
A rubber mat
Two long, heavy-duty zip ties
Scissors and a knife

Eye Safety
Danger to the eye; safety
goggles should be worn.

Instructions:

STEP 1: Using a knife, have an adult cut a five-inch hole in the center of the bottom of the bucket.

STEP 2: Have an adult also cut a large square shape out of the rubber mat. Make sure this square is large enough to stretch over the top of the bucket.

STEP 3: Stretch the rubber mat over the top of the bucket. Secure the rubber mat with the heavy-duty zip ties.

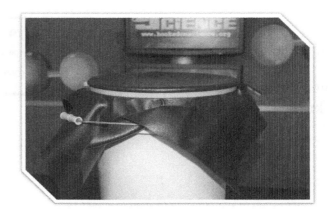

STEP 4: Point the end of the bucket that has the hole toward someone. Forcefully hit the rubber mat with the palm of your hand and observe.

Explanation

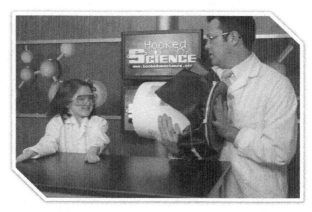

The air cannon proves that air takes up space. The rubber mat makes the shape of a cone as you forcefully hit it inward. The air pressure on the inside of the cannon increases and the air is forced into a rotating invisible rind as it moves through the five-inch hole and eventually hits someone or something with a force.

Bible Connection

We can't see air, but we know it's all around us when the wind mixes it up and it hits our skin. The same thing is true with the Holy Spirit. We can't see or touch the Holy Spirit but we can feel His presence in our hearts.

Science Terms

Air – Air is the mixture of gases that surrounds the earth.

Vortex – A vortex is a spinning mass of air, especially one in the form of a visible column or spiral, like a tornado.

SCIENCE QUIZ

1) Define air and vortex.

2) What does the air cannon prove?

3) What happens when you hit the rubber mat with the palm of your hand?

Patience

BIBLE TRUTH: *God rewards those that are patient.*

WHAT THE BIBLE SAYS: ***James 5:7***

7 Be patient, then, brothers and sisters, until the Lord's coming. See how the farmer waits for the land to yield its valuable crop, patiently waiting for the autumn and spring rains.

HANDS-ON EXPERIMENT: Skewer a Balloon

Ingredients:

Balloon
Skewer

Sharp Safety
Danger of cuts or
punctures .

Eye Safety
Danger to the eye; safety
goggles should be worn.

Instructions:

STEP 1: Ask and adult to blow up the balloon, let some of the air out and tie a knot at the end to hold the air inside the balloon.

STEP 2: Have an adult gently twist the skewer into one end of the balloon, near the knot. Continue to slowly push the skewer through the balloon until you push the skewer through the part opposite the knot.

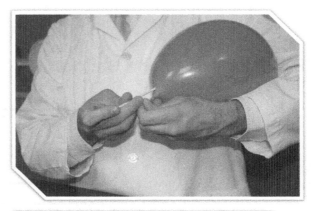

STEP 3: Have an adult pull the skewer out of the balloon and observe.

Explanation

The balloon is made up of polymers. These polymer strands seal up around the skewer, keeping the air from escaping and the balloon from popping. Once you pull the skewer out of the balloon, the air rushes out.

Bible Connection

With patience you were able to stick a skewer through a balloon. Learning to wait is a hard lesson in life, but the bible says that God rewards those who are patient.

Science Term

Polymer - A polymer is made up of many molecules linked together to form long chains.

SCIENCE QUIZ

1) Define polymer.

2) What kept the air from escaping when you pushed the skewer completely through the balloon?

3) What happened when you removed the skewer from the balloon?

How do you work on being patient?

Attract to God

BIBLE TRUTH: *Those who choose God will earn an ultimate strength.*

WHAT THE BIBLE SAYS: *Isaiah 40:31*

31 Those who hope in the Lord will renew their strength. They will soar on wings like eagles; they will run and not grow weary, they will walk and not be faint.

HANDS-ON EXPERIMENT: Magnetic Money

Ingredients:

Neodymium magnet
United States one dollar bill

Instructions:

STEP 1: Hold the dollar bill steadily, allowing the money to hang freely from your fingers.

STEP 2: Look for a place on the dollar bill that has a lot of ink. Bring the neodymium magnet close to the dollar and observe.

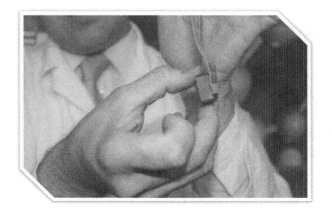

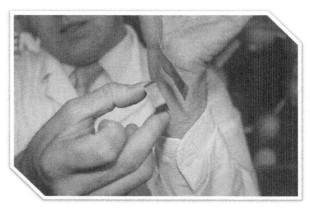

Explanation

The dollar was attracted to the strong magnet because of the ink. To prevent counterfeiting, dollar bills are printed with magnetic ink.

Bible Connection

We should attract to God like the dollar attracts to the strong magnet. When we do, we earn the ultimate strength.

48

Science Terms

Magnet – A magnet is an object that attracts specific types of metals.

Neodymium Magnet – Neodymium magnets are very strong in comparison to their mass, but are also mechanically fragile and the most powerful grades lose their magnetism at temperatures above 176 degrees Fahrenheit.

SCIENCE QUIZ

1) Define magnet and neodymium magnet.

2) Why was the dollar attracted to the strong magnet?

How is your heart attracted to God?

God's Voice

BIBLE TRUTH: *God's voice is more powerful than any you will ever hear.*

WHAT THE BIBLE SAYS: *Hebrews 4:12*

12 For the word of God is alive and active. Sharper than any double-edged sword, it penetrates even to dividing soul and spirit, joints and marrow; it judges the thoughts and attitudes of the heart.

HANDS-ON EXPERIMENT: Cup of Sounds

Ingredients:

Plastic cup
Sponge
String
Water
Scissors

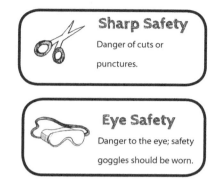

Sharp Safety
Danger of cuts or punctures.

Eye Safety
Danger to the eye; safety goggles should be worn.

Instructions:

STEP 1: Using a knife or scissors, have an adult create a small hole in the bottom of the plastic cup.

STEP 2: Have an adult cut about two feet of string and thread the string through the hole in the plastic cup.

STEP 3: Tie a knot in the string big enough so the string will not pull out of the hole in the plastic cup.

STEP 4: Wet the sponge, use it to grab the string close to the plastic cup, and then pull downward with the sponge.

Explanation

You created vibrations in the string by moving the wet sponge along the string. These vibrations produced sound, and the sound was amplified as it passed through the plastic cup.

Bible Connection

We could hear the unique sound loud and clear as the wet sponge moved along the sting, creating vibrations. Another sound we can hear loud and clear is God's voice. His voice is more powerful than anything you will ever hear.

Science Term

Sound – Sound is a type of energy that is created when an object vibrates.

SCIENCE QUIZ

1) Define sound.

2) What did you create when you moved the wet sponge along the string?

3) What amplified the sound?

The Ultimate Forecaster

BIBLE TRUTH: *God controls all weather and is the chief meteorologist.*

WHAT THE BIBLE SAYS: *Exodus 9:29*

29 Moses replied, "When I have gone out of the city, I will spread out my hands in prayer to the Lord. The thunder will stop and there will be no more hail, so you may know that the earth is the Lord's."

HANDS-ON EXPERIMENT: Cloud in a Bottle

Ingredients:

One two-liter clear plastic bottle
Water
Matches

Fire Safety
Care should be taken around open flames.

Eye Safety
Danger to the eye; safety goggles should be worn.

Instructions:

STEP 1: Add a small amount of water into the bottom of the plastic bottle.

STEP 2: Have an adult light a match and place the burning match into the bottle. Quickly screw the top on the plastic bottle.

STEP 3: Squeeze and release the plastic bottle several times, then observe.

Explanation

When the plastic bottle is released, the pressure and temperature decrease, which allows water vapor to condense on the smoke particles. When this occurs a cloud is created.

Bible Connection

Although we were able to create a cloud by using a specific set of ingredients and instructions, God controls all weather and is the chief meteorologist of Earth.

Science Terms

Cloud – A cloud is millions of tiny water droplets or ice crystals suspended in the air.

Condensation – Condensation occurs as water vapor cools and turns into drops of water.

SCIENCE QUIZ

1) Define cloud and condensation.

2) What happened when you released the plastic bottle?

Trust God

BIBLE TRUTH: *We cannot always choose the situation we are in, but we can always trust that God will guide us through anything.*

WHAT THE BIBLE SAYS: *Isaiah 43:10*

10 You are my witnesses, declares the Lord, and my servant whom I have chosen, so that you may know and believe me and understand that I am he. Before me no god was formed, nor will there be one after me.

HANDS-ON EXPERIMENT: Newton's Tablecloth

Ingredients:

Several heavy glass dishes
Tablecloth without a hem
Square table with an edge

Eye Safety

Danger to the eye; safety

goggles should be worn.

Instructions:

STEP 1: Place the tablecloth on the table and then arrange the glass dishes on the tablecloth.

STEP 2: Grab the edges of the tablecloth and pull down toward the floor quickly.

Explanation

The dishes stayed on the table as you quickly removed the tablecloth. This happened because of inertia. Inertia describes how an object will either keep moving or stay still unless an outside force acts on the object. The heavier an object is, the more inertia it has. This is the reason why plastic or paper dishes will not work for this experiment. They do not have enough inertia.

Bible Connection

This experiment took a lot of trust. You had to believe that you could pull the tablecloth from underneath the dishes without the dishes breaking. In life, we can't always choose the situation we are in, but we can always trust that God will guide us through anything.

Science Term

Inertia - Inertia describes how an object will either keep moving or stay still unless an outside force acts on the object.

SCIENCE QUIZ

1) Define inertia.

2) Why did the dishes stay on the table as you quickly removed the tablecloth?

How do you show your trust in God?

Father, Son and Holy Spirit

BIBLE TRUTH: *The Father, the Son and the Holy Spirit are each equally and eternally the one true God.*

WHAT THE BIBLE SAYS: *Matthew 28:19*

19 Therefore go and make disciples of all nations, baptizing them in the name of the Father and of the Son and of the Holy Spirit.

HANDS-ON EXPERIMENT: Dry Water

Ingredients:

Water
Ice cube tray

Instructions:

STEP 1: Pour the water into the ice cube tray.

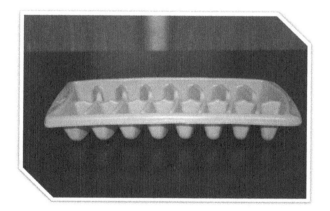

STEP 2: Place the ice cube tray into the freezer.

STEP 3: After several hours, remove the ice cube tray from the freezer and observe dry water.

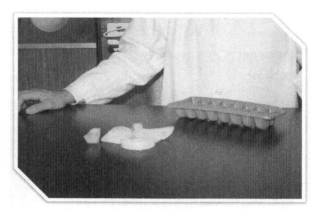

Explanation

Water can exist as a liquid, a solid or a gas. When you placed the ice cube tray in the freezer, the water froze. A solid, or dry water, was formed. If an adult brings a pan of water to a boil, the water goes from a liquid to a gas.

Bible Connection

Just as water can exist in three states, God exists as the Father, the Son and the Holy Spirit.

Science Terms

Temperature - Temperature is a measurement of how hot or cold an object is.

SCIENCE QUIZ

1) Define temperature.

2) What are the three states of water?

Science Dictionary

Air - Air is the mixture of gases that surrounds the earth.

Bernoulli's Principle - Bernoulli's principle states that the pressure exerted by a fluid decreases as its velocity increases.

Carbon Dioxide - Carbon dioxide is a colorless, odorless gas that animals breathe out as is naturally found in the air.

Chromophore - A chromophore is the part of a molecule responsible for its color.

Cloud - A cloud is millions of tiny water droplets or ice crystals suspended in the air.

Condensation - Condensation occurs as water vapor cools and turns into drops of water.

High Pressure System - A high-pressure system or an anticyclone is an area where the air diverges and sinks. A high-pressure system usually brings clear skies.

Inertia - Inertia describes how an object will either keep moving or stay still unless an outside force acts on the object.

Low Pressure System - A low-pressure system or cyclone is an area where the air converges and rises. A low-pressure system usually brings precipitation.

Magnet - A magnet is an object that attracts specific types of metals.

Molecule - A molecule is made up of two or more atoms that are joined together.

Neodymium Magnet - Neodymium magnets are very strong in comparison to their mass, but are also mechanically fragile and the most powerful grades lose their magnetism at temperatures above 176 degrees Fahrenheit.

Polymer - A polymer is made up of many molecules linked together to form long chains.

Sound - Sound is a type of energy that is created when an object vibrates.

Temperature - Temperature is a measurement of how hot or cold an object is.

Vortex - A vortex is a spinning mass of air, especially one in the form of a visible column or spiral, like a tornado.

The Bible and Science

Here are a few topics you might encounter while doing Beyond the Science lab experiments. You will discover specific Bible scripture below each topic indicating what the bible says about each topic.

Astronomy

Astronomy is the study of stars, planets and space. The solar system contains a variety of objects that revolve around the sun. The sun is the largest object in the solar system. There are eight planets in our solar system. The inner planets include Mercury, Venus, Earth and Mars. The outer planets include Jupiter, Saturn, Uranus and Neptune.

Amos 5:8
8 He who made the Pleiades and Orion, who turns midnight into dawn and darkens day into night, who calls for the waters of the sea

and pours them out over the face of the land—the Lord is his name.

Climate

Climate is the average weather in a specific area over an extended period of time. Climate affects the soil, the kinds of plants and animals in an ecosystem. There are many different climate zones around the world.

Genesis 8:22
22 As long as the earth endures, seedtime and harvest, cold and heat, summer and winter, day and night will never cease.

Clouds

A cloud is millions of tiny water droplets or ice crystals suspended in the air. The types of clouds in an area can help predict the weather. Clouds are classified by form and altitude. Cumulus clouds are puffy, white clouds. Stratus clouds from in layers. Cirrus clouds are thin, feathery clouds.

Job 26:8
8 He wraps up the waters in his clouds, yet the clouds do not burst under their weight.

Earthquake

Earthquakes happen when two plates smash and grind past each other. Most earthquakes happen along faults, which are huge cracks in the Earth's crust. A seismograph is an instrument used by scientists, which draws lines on a piece of paper. The lines indicate the strength of the waves created by the earthquake.

Isaiah 24:19-20
19 The earth is broken up, the earth is split asunder, the earth is violently shaken.
20 The earth reels like a drunkard, it sways like a hut in the wind; so heavy upon it is the guilt of its rebellion that it falls—never to rise again.

Eclipse

A solar eclipse happens when the moon comes between Earth and the sun and the shadow of the moon falls on part of Earth. A lunar eclipse happens when Earth comes between the sun and the moon and the shadow of Earth falls on the moon.

Amos 8:9
9 In that day, declares the Sovereign Lord, I will make the sun go down at noon and darken the earth in broad daylight.

Ecology

Ecology is how living things interact with other living things and their environment. Ecologists are scientists that study ecology.

Numbers 35:33-34
33 Do not pollute the land where you are. Bloodshed pollutes the land, and atonement cannot be made for the land on which blood has been shed, except by the blood of the one who shed it.
34 Do not defile the land where you live and where I dwell, for I, the Lord, dwell among the Israelites.

Weather Forecasting

A weather forecast is a prediction of specific weather conditions over the next 5 to 7 days. A meteorologist is a scientist who collects weather data to create weather forecasts. Meteorologists use weather balloons, thermometers, anemometers, barometers, wind vanes, Doppler Radar, satellites and forecasting models to create a forecast for a specific area.

Luke 12:54-56
54 He said to the crowd: When you see a cloud rising in the west, immediately you say, It's going to rain, and it does.
55 And when the south wind blows, you say, It's going to be hot, and it is.
56 Hypocrites! You know how to interpret the appearance of the earth and the sky. How is it that you don't know how to interpret this present time?

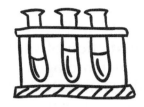

Science Questions Kids Ask

Kids can ask what seems like a thousand tough questions a day. If you find yourself wondering how to respond or even explain an answer to a question your child has asked, here are the answers to some of the most common questions that kids have asked me during these experiments.

GOD GIVES US POWER

How do airplanes fly?

Airplane's wings are flat on the bottom and curved at the top. Due to this unique shape, airplanes are able to lift and stay in the air. Bernoulli's Principle states that the pressure exerted by a fluid decreases as its velocity increases. Increasing the velocity over the top surface of the wings lowers the pressure of the air pushing down on the wings. The airplane is lifted because there is now an unbalanced force of air pressure acting upward.

GOD' POWER

What is a 35mm film canister?

A 35mm film canister is a container made specifically for photographic film. Those taking pictures using photographic film return their exposed film in the container for processing.

SQUEAKY CLEAN HEART

What is soap made of?

Originally soap was created by boiling lard or other animal fat together with lye or potassium hydroxide. Nowadays, the main ingredients required to manufacture soap are animal fat or vegetable oil, sodium hydroxide and sodium chloride.

GOD'S LIGHT

What causes a rainbow?

As the light from the sun passes through water droplets, which act as tiny prisms, the light is bent into separate wavelengths. When these wavelengths are separated, each one corresponds to a specific color. The rainbow is made up of seven colors. These colors always appear in the same order. An easy way to remember these colors is to remember the first letter of each color. This spells out "Roy G Biv." The letter R represents red, O represents orange, Y represents yellow, G represents green, B represents blue, I represents indigo and V represents violet. You see most rainbows late in the day because the sun must be near the horizon for a rainbow to appear.

PATIENCE

What are some examples of polymers?

A polymer is made up of many molecules linked together to form long chains. There are many natural and synthetic polymers. Plastics are the most common example of synthetic polymers. Other examples of synthetic polymers include silly putty, Styrofoam cups and rubber. Proteins, such as hair, nails and a tortoise shell are examples of natural polymers.

THE ULTIMATE FORECASTER

Why is the sky blue?

The light from the sun consists of different wavelengths and when these wavelengths are separated, each one corresponds to a specific color. As sunlight reaches the Earth's atmosphere it's scattered in all directions. The color blue is scattered more than any of the colors since it travels in shorter, smaller waves. Therefore, we see the sky as blue.

FATHER, SON, AND HOLY SPIRIT

At what temperature does water boil and at what temperature does water freeze?

Temperature is a measurement of how hot or cold an object is. Water boils at a temperature of 212 degrees Fahrenheit or 100 degrees Celsius and freezes at a temperature of 32 degrees Fahrenheit or zero degrees Celsius.

As a parent you want to encourage these questions, and more. Questions will help your child become a strong thinker.

About the Author

Jason Lindsey is an award-winning outreach science educator. Jason studied science and journalism at Western Kentucky University where he earned a Bachelor of Science degree. At Western Kentucky University, Jason focused on general science with an emphasis on meteorology and climatology. Jason has worked diligently for more than ten years to take science beyond the classroom window. Each year he performs hands-on science experiments at hundreds of schools and community events.

Jason previously worked as a meteorologist, backpack journalist, science reporter and webmaster at WKAG-TV, WBKO-TV, KGWN-TV and KFVS-TV. Jason now produces a science segment called "Hooked on Science." The segment airs on television stations across the nation and has earned awards for outstanding science coverage.

On October 3, 2009 Jason organized "Science Day 2009." During the event hundreds of kids, young and old, set a world record by participating in the largest chemistry lesson. At Science Day 2008, the residents of southeast Missouri, southern Illinois, and western Kentucky blew up 852 balloons in an hour breaking the previous record of 600 balloons. During Science Day 2007 folks from across southeast Missouri launched more than 1000 "Mentos and soda fountains" breaking the previous record of more than 800 launched in the Netherlands.

Jason and his wife, Lena, have been married for more than ten years. They keep busy with their four kids Conner, Ethan, Brynna, and Madigan.

Jason's Picks

Here are some of Jason's favorite places to visit for hands-on science resources:

Educational Innovations *(http://www.teachersource.com)*
For teachers, master educators, and budding scientists, Educational Innovations is the source for inexpensive and hard-to-find science experiments, science fair projects and supplies, and teaching and learning materials. Educational Innovations has everything needed for the lab, classroom, or workshop of the school, university and home experimenter.

Giant Microbes *(http://www.giantmicrobes.com)*
Most folks never realize how cute microbes can be when expanded 1,000,000 times and then fashioned into cuddly plush. Until now, that is. Keep one on your desktop to remind yourself that there is an "invisible" universe out there filled with very small things that can do incredible damage to much bigger things.

Homeschool Channel *(http://www.thehomeschoolchannel.tv)*
The Homeschool Channel is an Internet Protocol Television (IPTV) project of The American Family Association. The Homeschool Channel is devoted to encouraging parents with the day-to-day challenges of home education and family discipleship. The Homeschool Channel website is a free community of homeschooling families sharing videos, blogs and discussions.

Laser Pegs *(http://www.laserpegs.com)*
The national award winning Laser Pegs is the first unique toy construction set in the world in which each piece feeds low voltage current to the next piece. They can be used to design and build any lighted abstract model. Laser Pegs can be used lit up or turned off. Once one Laser Peg is connected

to a power source it illuminates any other peg it is connected with, making this a very creative construction toy set.

Learning Resources *(http://www.learningresources.com)*
Learning Resources is a leading manufacturer of learning toys and innovative hands-on educational materials for classrooms worldwide. For 25 years, Learning Resources has been a trusted source for teachers and parents for quality, award-winning educational products in math, science, social studies, language, language arts, literacy, reading, early childhood, Spanish, ELL and ESL teaching, classroom management, response to intervention (RTI) and professional development (PD).

SchoolhouseTeachers.com *(http://www.schoolhouseteachers.com)*
Schoolhouseteachers.com was created with the vision to provide quality homeschool materials from the best teachers, nationally and internationally, in many subject areas. They offer daily, weekly and monthly lesson plans and activity ideas. Their teachers provide weekly or monthly activities that you can use at your convenience with your own lesson plans. More than a dozen unit studies—art, theater, grammar, spelling, writing, and more—also are included. You also will receive daily historical information, daily menu ideas and tons more.

The Old Schoolhouse Magazine for Homeschool Families *(www.TOSMagazine.com)*
The Old Schoolhouse® Magazine is the premier, monthly homeschooling magazine worldwide! Packed full (over 150 pages per month) of encouraging and informative content, TOS brings you the biggest names in homeschooling all in one place.

Where to Watch Hooked on Science

KRCG 13 — SUN 7am
13 WIBW-TV — SAT 8am
WPSD LOCAL 6 — SAT 8am
TCT KIDS — SAT

CBS 5 NewsChannel — WED 12pm
BOWLING GREEN'S NBC 40 WNKY-DT 40.1 — WED 6:30am
LOCAL 7 WTVW — WED 8am
LIFESTYLE CTN Family Television — SAT

The Hooked on Science television segment continues to get kids, young and old, "Hooked on Science" around the world. Look for the segment on DirectTV, Cable Television, TCT World, Sky Angel, the Homeschool Channel, and television stations across America during local news and children's programming.

Pinwheel Books

Pinwheel Books is a small publisher of children's books located in Brookline, MA. To learn more about our books, including our hit book "All About Poop," whose teacher and parent guide was developed by Hooked On Science, visit www.pinwheelbooks.com.

CPSIA information can be obtained at www.ICGtesting.com
Printed in the USA
LVOW020348091212

310707LV00001B/1/P